General editor
DIANA ZAFEIROPOULOU

Textual editing
ELENI KOTSOU

Artistic supervision
VANA MARI

Translation
ALEXANDRA DOUMAS

Photographs
ARCHIVE OF THE ARCHAEOLOGICAL RECEIPTS FUND
(M. Skiadaresis - G. Fafalis - I. Georgouleas - Kl.-V. von Eickstedt)

Typesetting
KATERINA ILIOPOULOU

Reproduction
K. ADAM

Printing
PERGAMOS SA

5th edition 2007 (2000[1])

© 2007
ARCHAEOLOGICAL RECEIPTS FUND
PUBLICATIONS DEPARTMENT
57 Panepistimiou St., Athens 105 64
www.tap.gr

ISBN 978-960-214-448-0

HELLENIC MINISTRY OF CULTURE
ARCHAEOLOGICAL RECEIPTS FUND

THE NATIONAL

ARCHAEOLOGICAL MUSEUM

ATHENS 2007

THE NATIONAL
ARCHAEOLOGICAL
MUSEUM

Brief History

When the wind of freedom began to blow for the Greeks, after the 1821 War of Independence, the need to rescue the monuments – especially the moveable ones – which had survived the predations and were dispersed in every corner of Greek territory, soon became felt. Thus, the first museum, which housed mainly sculptures, was founded in 1829, on the island of Aegina, first capital of the Modern Greek State. After the transfer of the capital to Athens and due to the growing number of finds, the Central Archaeological Museum was established in 1834, which was accommodated temporarily in the temple of Hephaistos, popularly known as the Theseion.

However, the rapid increase in the number of objects brought to light in excavations, mainly conducted by the Archaeological Society, necessitated the construction of a large, purpose-built museum. The site of this building was provided by Eleni Tositsa, who donated to the Greek State a plot of land situated between Patision, Vasileos Irakleiou, Bouboulinas and Tositsa streets. Of decisive importance for the erecting of the museum was the sponsorship of the great Greek expatriate benefactor Demetrios Bernardakis, domiciled in St Petersburg, who at that time (1857-1858) offered the sum of two hundred thousand drachmas.

The foundation stone was laid on 3 October 1866 and building began to plans prepared by Ludwig Lange. In 1871 Nikolaos Bernardakis, son of the late Demetrios, provided one hundred thousand francs for the project to continue.

In the meantime, Ernst Ziller had modified Lange's original designs, abolishing the large colonnade on the façade and creating an Ionic propylon flanked by two closed stoas with openings in the form of big windows. The final building phases were completed gradually, until 1885.

By Royal Decree of 19 April 1881, the Central Archaeological Museum was renamed the National Archaeological Museum. All the antiquities which had been gathered and stored until then in various other buildings, such as the Theseion, the Stoa of Hadrian, the Tower of the Winds, the Varvakeion, the Kerameikos and the Polytechneion, were transferred to the new premises. The Museum has been enriched since the nineteenth century to this day with a host of objects, both from excavations and donations, such as those made by I. Demetriou, A. Rostovitz, I. Misthos, K. Karapanos, G. Empedokles, H. Stathatou, L. Benakis, I.P. Serpieri-Vlastos and others.

In 1925 the decision was taken to expand the Museum premises, and between 1932 and 1939 the new two-storey wing to the east of the old building, facing Bouboulinas street, was erected to plans by G. Nomikos.

However, as fate would have it, the new exhibition of antiquities was not installed in this section, because war was declared in October 1940. During the hostilities between Greece and Italy and the subsequent German Occupation of Greece, the National Archaeological Museum lived its own dramatic story.

In order to protect its precious contents from the invaders and from bombardments, large-scale concealment works were carried out, which lasted almost six months, that is as long as the Greek Army was able to defend the Greek-Albanian border.

All the small precious objects and gold items were packed in boxes and hidden in the vaults of the Bank of Greece. Several sculptures were removed and protected in natural hideouts away from Athens. However, most of the sculptures and vases were hidden in the basements of the museum itself. The pottery was packed carefully in wooden cases, while special measures were taken for the bronzes, which were placed in cases specially insulated against damp. The large bronze sculptures were wrapped like mummies in tarpaulin, for the same reason.

In order to hide the large marble statues, pits were opened beneath the exhibition galleries, causing the destruction of the ornate mosaic floors. All the basements of the newly-built wing were filled with antiquities, which were covered with enormous quantities of dry sand. Sandbags were also stacked along the length of all the windows of the basements, for protection in the event of bombardment.

Following the retreat of the occupation forces, the building functioned as a detention centre during the Civil War, at the end of which it was severely damaged and left roofless, due to bombs.

Work on restoring the building, in parallel with work on bringing to light the antiquities and re-exhibiting them, commenced in 1946. In 1950 the first temporary exhibition was inaugurated in six galleries of the museum. The permanent exhibition of its collections was completed in stages between 1950 and 1966. It was rather *avant-garde* in form and the style for the time, since it deviated appreciably from the ethos of the rest of the museums in Europe.

The Museum displays retained this aspect for almost 40 years, despite minor interventions made from time to time by the keepers of the various collections.

From the 1990s, however, the need to reorganize the exhibition in the museum was strongly felt and in the end became imperative. In 1994 the Egyptian Collection was re-exhibited, in 1996 the Roman Sculptures and in 2000 the Stathatos Collection. The first essential and large-scale re-exhibition in the main body of the permanent galleries was mounted in 2000, in the Sculpture Collection, and specifically in the north wing, with works of the Archaic and Early Classical periods.

The damage caused to the fabric of the building by the earthquake in September 1999, occasioned the preparation of a study for the renovation of the Museum as well as for the new exhibition of its collections.

The overall exhibition programme was drafted in 2002 and implemented between 2003 and 2005.

NIKOLAOS KALTSAS
Director of the National Archaeological Museum

The prehistoric collections of the National Archaeological Museum are displayed in four galleries (3-6) on the ground floor and in gallery 48 on the first floor. Most of the exhibits in these galleries come from the most important centres in the prehistoric Aegean world – Thessaly, the Cyclades and Mycenae –, where three of the most important cultures of prehistoric Greece developed and flourished from the early 7th millennium to 1100 BC. These are respectively the Neolithic (gallery 5), the Cycladic (gallery 6) and the Mycenaean (galleries 3 and 4) culture. In gallery 48 on the first floor are the famous wall-paintings and other artefacts from the site at Akrotiri on Thera (Santorini) (16th c. BC).

Globular vase with painted decoration in "scraped technique". Lianokladi, Phthiotis. Middle Neolithic period, 5800-5400 BC (no. 8051).

Closed globular vase with brownish black and red burnished paint. The elaborate linear decoration is the same on both sides. Citadel of Dimini. Late Neolithic period, 5300-4800 BC (no. 5922).

Large clay vase (hydria), one of the best examples of Urfirnis ware. The pot is also decorated with a ridge and incisions. Orchomenos, Boeotia. Early Bronze Age (EH II), 2900-2300 BC (no. 5877).

THE NEOLITHIC COLLECTION

"Krateutes". Clay quadrilateral stand with painted spiral decoration. Citadel of Sesklo. Late Neolithic period, 4800-4500 BC (no. 5935).

Gallery 5 hosts the earliest artefacts in the National Archaeological Museum, dating from the Neolithic Age (6800-3300 BC). During this stage man developed the skills of agriculture and animal husbandry and began to live in permanent settlements, three factors that shaped his new relationship with the environment and laid the foundations of the contemporary economy. Objects of clay and stone surviving from this culture in Neolithic settlements, yield direct information on the everyday activities of Neolithic man, as well as indirect on his ideological and religious beliefs and practices.
The artefacts in Gallery 5 are from two large settlements in Thessaly, Sesklo, which flourished during the Middle Neolithic, and Dimini, which was in its heyday in the Late Neolithic, as well as from Lianokladi in Phthiotis and Ales in Locris. They are clay vases and vessels, clay and stone figurines, and obsidian, stone and bone tools. Gallery 5 also includes objects of the Early (3rd mil-

"Thinker". Large clay ithyphallic figurine of a seated male figure. Karditsa area. Final Neolithic period, 4500-3300 BC (no. 5894).

lennium BC) and the Middle (2000-1700 BC) Bronze Age. The Bronze Age, which succeeded the Neolithic, is thus named because the use of metals, primarily bronze, became generalized.

The Early Bronze Age in the Greek mainland, known conventionally as the Early Helladic period (3300-2100/2000 BC), is represented by exhibits from Orchomenos in Boeotia, Rafina, Askitario and Aghios Kosmas in Attica, Poliochni on Lemnos, as well as cities II-V at Troy (finds donated by Sophia Schliemann). Also from Orchomenos, as well as Sesklo, Dimini and Lianokladi, are objects dated in the Middle Bronze Age or Middle Helladic period, the most characteristic of which are the so-called Minyan Ware vases.

ALEXANDRA CHRISTOPOULOU

Naturalistic marble female figurine with headdress and incised motifs on the arms. Sparta. Early Neolithic period, 6500-5800 BC (no. 3928).

"Kourotrophos". Clay figurine of a seated female embracing a child. Citadel of Sesklo. Late Neolithic period, 4800-4500 BC (no. 5937).

THE CYCLADIC COLLECTION

Exhibited in Gallery 6 are creations of the culture that developed in the Cyclades during the Bronze Age (3rd-2nd millennium BC). The majority were discovered in excavations conducted in these islands by Christos Tsountas, who in fact coined the term Cycladic Culture.

There are abundant finds from cemeteries and settlements of the Early Cycladic period (3rd millennium BC), when Cycladic culture was at its zenith and the islands were of seminal significance for developments in the Aegean region, with a remarkable development of metallurgy, shipbuilding and seafaring. Characteristic objects are the famous marble figurines and vases, the bronze tools and weapons. Outstanding are the three-dimensional figurines of musicians, in which the sculptors have mastered space,

Marble statue of a female figure of the characteristic type with folded arms. The largest extant example of Early Cycladic sculpture (h. 1.50 m). Amorgos. Early Cycladic II period, 2800-2300 BC (no. 3978).

Marble violin-shaped figurine. Paros. Early Cycladic I period, 3200-2800 BC (no. 4765).

Marble collared jar, known as a "kandila". Paros. Early Cycladic I period, 3200-2800 BC (no. 4759).

Marble figurine of a musician, holding a lyre or harp. The three-dimensional development of the figure in space bears witness to the early development of Cycladic sculpture. Keros. Early Cycladic II period, 2800-2300 BC (no. 3908).

Clay "frying-pan" vessel with incised representation of a ship. Chalandriani cemetery, Syros. Early Cycladic II period, 2800-2300 BC (no. 4974).

and the statue of the female figure with folded arms, a monumental sculpture of Early Cycladic times. Likewise well known are the marble collared jars, popularly known as "kandiles" (i.e. icon lamps), the violin-shaped figurines and the singular clay "frying-pan" vessels with incised representations of ships, a very important source of information on the kinds of vessels ploughing the seas at this time.

The abundance of categories and types of bronze tools reveals the advances made in metalworking and the degree of craft specialization. Particularly interesting for the development of metal technology are the moulds, crucibles, slag and hammers found at Kastri on Syros, a representative Early Cycladic fortified hilltop settlement (Early Cycladic II-III period, 2nd half of 3rd millennium BC).

Also on display are important finds from the four suc-

Various types of bronze tools. Naxos. Early Cycladic II period, 2800-2300 BC.

cessive cities at Phylakopi on Melos (2300-1100 BC), which was enhanced as one of the most important centres in the Cyclades. Pottery with incised or painted motifs, geometric or pictorial (birds, animals and, even more fascinating, humans), as well as wall-paintings with naturalistic pictorial representations – those with lilies and with flying fish are among the best known – give an idea of the culture that developed in the Early, Middle and Late Cycladic Period, not only on Melos but in the Cyclades generally. Melos, source of obsidian – the volcanic glass from which chipped stone tools were made in the Aegean region from as early as the 8th millennium BC – was home to a culture whose influence was far reaching and which had overt influences from the Minoan and Mycenaean cultures during the Late Bronze Age.

ELENI TSIVILIKA

Clay jug with red and black painted depiction of a bird. Phylakopi. First half of 16th c. BC (no. 5762).

Wall-painting depicting a marine environment with flying fish. Phylakopi III. Mid-16th c. BC (no. 5844).

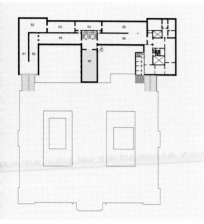

THERA

The Thera Gallery (Gallery 48) houses finds from the important settlement at Akrotiri on Thera, which was buried beneath pumice and pozzuolana by the volcanic eruption of the island in the late 16th c. BC.

There is considerable evidence that Thera was inhabited from the Late Neolithic period and subsequently followed the historical and cultural developments of the rest of the Cyclades.

The flourishing harbour town at Akrotiri was one of the major centres in the prehistoric Aegean enjoying an economic, social and cultural development on a par with that of Minoan Crete, with which it had close contacts

Wall-painting of antelopes. Detail from a large composition with six antelopes. 16th c. BC (BE 1974.26α).

The "Boxing Children" wall-painting. 16th c. BC (BE 1974.26b).

The "Spring" wall-painting, depicting the pre-eruption landscape of Thera, with red lilies growing from the tops and sides of the volcanic rocks, and playful swallows kissing in mid-air. 16th c. BC (BE 1974.29).

"Kymbe", a clay vase of unknown function, decorated with painted dolphins (no. 3266).

and by which it was influenced. The circulation of goods and the wealth of the inhabitants bear witness to a comfortable and refined lifestyle, such as that in the Minoan centres.

Masterworks of Aegean art are the wall-paintings that adorned some of the rooms in the houses and which have been preserved in excellent condition on account of the eruption. Of interest are the subjects of these pictorial compositions, which are drawn from Minoan models but also incorporate clear Cycladic elements. In several representations secular themes predominate, whereas others have a religious character. The abundant and important pottery finds at Akrotiri attest on the one hand close relations with Crete and contacts with Mycenaean Greece, and on the other the continuation of the rich, local, pictorial tradition.

DIMITRA KOKKEVI-PHOTIOU

Breasted jug decorated with bands, dots and eye motifs. 16th c. BC (no. 877).

Jug painted with polychrome birds. 16th c. BC (no. 1838).

Jug decorated with plant and eye motifs. 16th c. BC (no. 1470).

Clay strainer painted with lilies. 16th c. BC (no. 562).

THE MYCENAEAN COLLECTION

The Mycenaean Collection occupies the largest, central gallery in the Museum (Gallery 4) and extends into the smaller side gallery (Gallery 3). The exhibits present a vivid picture of Mycenaean Civilization, one of the most splendid cultures in prehistoric Greece, following its progress from its appearance in the early 16th c. BC to its demise in the 11th c. BC, that is covering the whole duration of the Late Bronze Age in the Aegean. Mycenaean Civilization was at its zenith during the 14th and 13th centuries BC, having first received the fertilizing influence of Minoan Crete. It is distinguished by its social and political organization, the monumental arts, advanced technology, development of communications through trade with virtually the entire Mediterranean, as well as the use of script to serve the palatial system of government, modelled on the Minoan. Mycenaean writing, known to scholarship as Linear

Stone grave stele with relief scene of battle or hunt from a chariot. Mycenae, Grave Circle A. 16th c. BC (no. 1428).

Gold signet-ring with representation of a goddess and daemons on the bezel. Citadel of Tiryns. c. 1500 BC (no. 6208).

Gold signet-ring with scene of deer hunt from a chariot on the bezel. Mycenae, Grave Circle A, Shaft Grave IV. 16th c. BC (no. 240).

Sandonyx, lentoid sealstone in a gold mount, with chariot scene. Vapheio, Tholos Tomb. 15th c. BC (no. 1770).

Head of a sphinx or a goddess in lime-plaster, with facial features picked out in colour. Citadel of Mycenae, Cult Centre. 13th c. BC (no. 4575).

B, is an early form of the Greek language. In addition to Mycenae, which was the mightiest centre, Mycenaean Civilization had several other important centres to its credit, the best known of which are Tiryns, Argos, Midea, Vapheio, Pylos, Thebes, Orchomenos, Athens, Thorikos and Iolkos.

The Mycenaean Collection includes a large number of works of art and other artefacts, discovered at important Mycenaean centres in the Aegean. Most of them were found in tombs and include exquisite examples of metalworking, glyptics, jewellery, sculpture and stone-carving, ivory-carving and painting in Mycenaean times. Mycenae's superiority in mainland Greece is evident in the exhibition, since over half the finds displayed were recovered from there. The rest were found at various sites in the Peloponnese, Attica, Thessaly and the Sporades, as well as the island of Kythera.

The exhibit, which is developed thematically and according to the geographical provenance of the objects, begins from the central gallery of the Museum with finds from the excavations at Mycenae. To the fore are the treasures from the shaft graves of Grave Circles A and B (16th c. BC), with first the stone funerary stelae, which were set up on the graves. Outstanding among the treasures are the famous funerary masks of beaten-gold sheet that covered the face

Gold cup with two handles crowned by doves. Mycenae, Grave Circle A, Shaft Grave IV. 16th c. BC (no. 412).

Gold cup with representation of a marine environment. Dendra, Tholos Tomb. 15th c. BC (no. 7341).

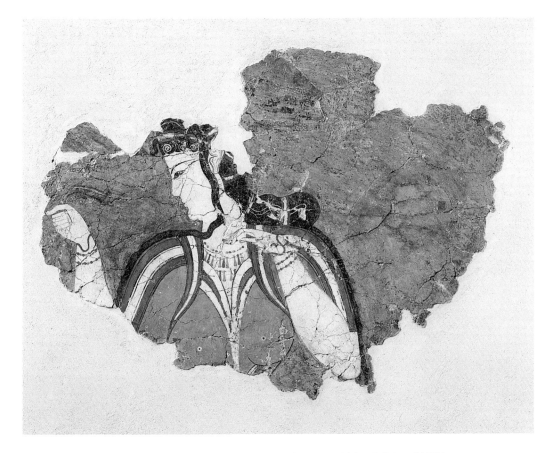

Wall-painting depicting a goddess. Citadel of Mycenae, Cult Centre. 13th c. BC (no. 11670).

of the dead Mycenaean rulers, finely worked vases of gold, silver, rock crystal and alabaster, large bronze vessels and precious jewellery, such as gold diadems and crowns, necklaces, dress pins and signet-rings. There are also many weapons, the most important of which are bronze daggers with beautiful pictorial representations inlaid in gold, silver and niello. Next come finds from the tholos and the chamber tombs at Mycenae, such as stone, metal and clay vases, clay figurines, including the renowned "kourotrophos", ivories, seals and jewellery of gold, semiprecious stones, glass and faience (15th-13th c. BC). The finds from the citadel of Mycenae itself include

Rock crystal bowl in the form of a duck. Mycenae, Grave Circle B, Shaft Grave O. Early 16th c. BC (no. 8638).

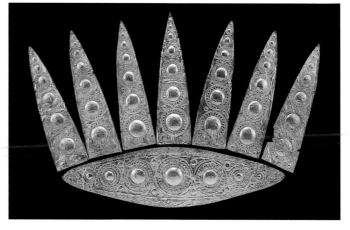

Gold diadem. Mycenae, Grave Circle A, Shaft Grave III. 16th c. BC (no. 1).

Gold funerary mask. Mycenae, Grave Circle A, Shaft Grave V. 16th c. BC (no. 624).

Silver pin with gold head in the form of a female figure holding papyrus branches. Mycenae, Grave Circle A, Shaft Grave III. 16th c. BC (no. 75).

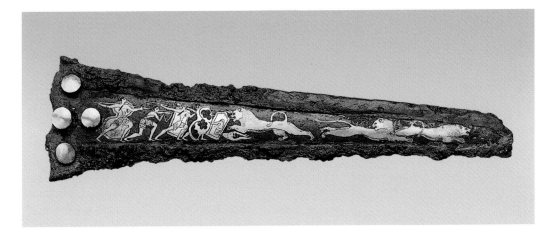

Bronze dagger with inlaid representation of a lion hunt in gold, silver and niello. Mycenae, Grave Circle A, Shaft Grave IV. 16th c. BC (no. 394).

remarkable works of art, among them gold and stone vases, a head of a sphinx or a goddess in lime-plaster with painted details, the "warrior krater" and the ivory group of two female deities with a young god between them (15th-12th c. BC). Extremely important are the wall-paintings from the "Cult Centre" at Mycenae (13th c. BC). The remaining section of the Mycenaean exhibition in the central hall is given over to finds from other major Mycenaean centres in the Argolid, such as Tiryns and Dendra, as well as from Pylos and Vapheio. Among the precious finds from the citadel of Tiryns

Gold cups with repoussé scenes of capturing bulls. Vapheio, Tholos Tomb. 15th c. BC (nos 1758, 1759).

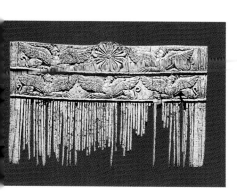

Ivory comb with relief decoration of sphinxes. Spata, Attica, Chamber Tomb. 13th c. BC (no. 2044).

is the famous gold signet-ring with an engraved representation of a religious scene (c. 1500 BC). The rich objects dicovered in the Mycenaean cemetery at Dendra include copious gold, silver and bronze vessels, gold jewellery and sealstones. Famous is the gold cup with the repoussé representation of a marine environment (15th c. BC). The valuable artefacts from the Palace and Tholos Tombs of Pylos are particularly interesting, among them the rich palatial archive of clay Linear B tablets (13th c. BC). Renowned too are the finds from the Tholos Tomb at Vapheio in Laconia (15th c. BC), outstanding among which are the two gold cups with repoussé scenes of capturing bulls, and

Ivory head of a warrior with boar's tusk helmet. Mycenae, Chamber Tomb 27. 14th-13th c. BC (no. 2468).

Ivory group of two sitting female deities with a young god between them. Citadel of Mycenae, Palace area. 15th c. BC (no. 7711).

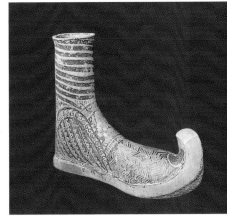

the large collection of sealstones with various engraved scenes.
The Mycenaean exhibition concludes in the small side
Gallery 3, where finds from important Mycenaean
centres of Central Greece and the Aegean islands are
exhibited (15th-11th c. BC): Ivories, jewellery of gold
and other materials from tombs at Spata and Menidi
in Attica, clay vases and figurines, jewellery, weapons
and tools from Thorikos, Marathon, Athens, Voula,
Perati, Aegina and Salamis, as well as gold jewellery,
a gold sword hilt, bronze and clay vases from Thessaly,
Skopelos and Kythera.

KATIE DEMAKOPOULOU

*Clay figurine of a kourotrophos (mother
and child). Mycenae, Chamber Tomb 41.
14th c. BC (no. 2493).*

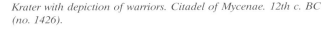

*Krater with depiction of warriors. Citadel of Mycenae. 12th c. BC
(no. 1426).*

*Clay boot model with denticulated dec-
oration on the ankles, perhaps denoting
wings. Voula, Attica, Chamber Tomb.
14th c. BC (no. 8557).*

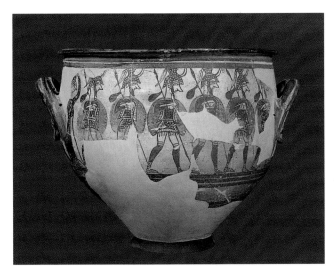

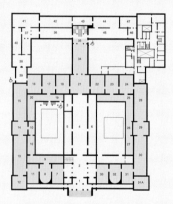

The sculpture collection of the National Archaeological Museum covers the historical period, from the 7th c. BC until Late Antiquity. This treasure trove of monumental sculpted works unfolds in 30 galleries on the ground floor of the Museum, following a circuitous route in chronological sequence. The visitor begins the tour in Gallery 7, to the left of the entrance hall, with the earliest works of monumental sculpture, and continues round the perimeter of the original Museum building, ending in gallery 33 with the works of Late Antiquity. The piecemeal representation of different regions of Greece, which is apparent to the visitor as he tours the galleries, is not only due to practical reasons – the difficulty or ease with which works could be transported to Athens when the archaeologists were assembling the exhibits for the National Museum in the early 20th century. It also undoubtedly reflects the actual situation in various cities in Antiquity. For example, the predominance of Athens in this exhibition is justified by the fact that this metropolis of intellectual and cultural achievement had a long tradition in this sector of art and a formidable output of sculpted works.

All kinds of sculptures, reliefs and statues in the round, are exhibited in chronological order so that the visitor can appreciate their development

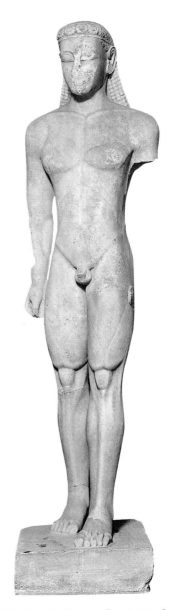

from the first austere and conventional formats of the Archaic period to the realistic, pathos-filled figures of Hellenistic times and the rendering of personal features in the portraits of the Roman era. It is also noted that many sculptures belong to ensembles, such as for example the votive reliefs from the Asklepieion at Athens, the sculptures from the decoration of the temple of Asklepios at Epidauros and so on. The development of sculpture through time is divided by art historians into four major periods, which coincide with corresponding historical periods defined by important events that gave each its particular social, political and artistic milieu. These periods are: the Archaic (7th c. - 480 BC, that is the end of the Persian Wars), the Classical (480 BC - Alexander the Great), the Hellenistic (death of Alexander the Great - subjugation of the last Hellenistic kingdom, of the Ptolemies, to the Romans) and Roman (reign of Octavian Augustus - founding of the Byzantine state and the prevailing of Christianity).

The Sounion kouros. Sanctuary of Poseidon at Sounion. c. 600 BC (no. 2720).

Kouros. Volomandra, the Mesogeia in Attica. 560-550 BC (no. 1906).

The kore Phrasikleia. Merenda in Attica. 550-540 BC (no. 4889).

Gallery 7

Exhibited here are works in the so-called "Daedalic style", thus named after the mythical sculptor Daedalus, which are the precursors of Archaic art. Outstanding are the poros reliefs from the temple of Athena at Mycenae and three statues of seated female figures. An exemplar of the Daedalic style is the female statue no. 1, which was dedicated by a Naxian lady, Nikandre, to the goddess Artemis on Delos. Found on the sacred isle of Apollo, in the *oikos* of the Naxians, and dated around 650 BC, it is the earliest known life-size stone statue in Greece and probably represents Artemis herself.

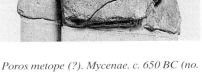

Poros metope (?). Mycenae. c. 650 BC (no. 2869).

Galleries 8-13

These six galleries house Archaic sculptures, dating from the 7th c. till 480 BC. Of the two most important and characteristic statue types of this period, the *kouros* and the *kore*, the former predominates in the Museum.

The Hoplitodromos relief. Athens. c. 500 BC (no. 1959).

The colossal kouros no. 2720, from the sanctuary of Poseidon at Sounion, is an example of these imposing works which were set up in sanctuaries as *ex-votos* or on graves as funerary statues.
Exhibited in Gallery 11 is a kouros from the Cycladic island of Melos (no. 1558), dated around 560 BC. He stands tall and slender, almost feeble, facing the world with sensitivity, in contrast to his robust counterparts from Attica.
The loveliest kore in the National Museum is Phrasikleia (no. 4889), who is imbued with the grief felt at the untimely death of the maiden on whose grave it once stood, to remind passers-by of her lost beauty.
The erecting of grave markers is a practice known since at least Mycenaean times. From the 7th c. BC the monumental clay funerary amphorae and kraters of the Geometric period were replaced by funerary stelae, which gradually acquired a monu-

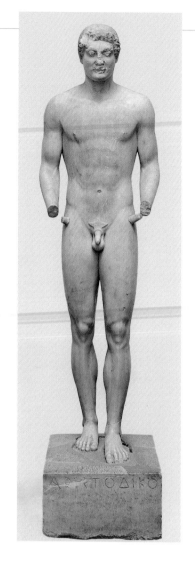

Aristodikos. Mesogeia in Attica. 510-500 BC (no. 3938).

mental form, developing from simple pillars into elaborate masterpieces with relief representations and capitals, which are usually adorned with sedent sphinxes. Examples of such stelae are displayed in Gallery 11. Outstanding for the quality of its workmanship is stele fragment no. 38, with the profile head of a young discophoros, admirably projected against the circular shape of the discus.

The series of kouroi continues with the kouros from Volomandra, Mesogeia in Attica (no. 1906) in Gallery 11, and from Kea (no. 3686) in Gallery 13. Clearly visible in the second piece are the advances made in the rendering of the human body, particularly of the facial features; the artist begins to integrate them into an organic whole rather than to treat them as separate elements on the human head, as in the early kouroi. Noteworthy too in this gallery is the funerary stele of a warrior (no. 29), dated around 500 BC, from Velanideza in Attica.

The relief of the *Hoplitodromos* (no. 1959) in Gallery 13 is a fine example of the incorporation of a male figure in movement within the confines of the peculiar trapezoidal stele. The nude youth in helmet, possibly a dancer performing the *pyrrhicheion*, runs right with his body en face and his head turned behind.

Works of the Late Archaic period are exhibited in Gallery 13, among them the latest kouroi. Kouros no. 3851, from Anavyssos, sturdy with pronounced musculature, was erected on the grave of a young man named Kroisos, who died in war, as is recorded in the incised inscription on the plinth.

Outstanding among the ensemble of kouroi found in the sanctuary of Apollo at Ptoon in Boeotia is no. 20, with the arms bent and in frontward motion. The last Attic kouros, which sets its seal on the Archaic period and opens the way for Classical sculpture, is Aristodikos (no. 3938), dated around 510-500 BC. This funerary statue is liberated from the strictures of the Archaic canons. The hair is short, possibly coloured originally, the arms are free and the musculature of the body is modelled with plasticity and soft volumes, while nowhere are there the linear grooves observed

Fragment of a funerary stele, with a youth holding a discus. Dipylon. c. 550 BC (no. 38).

on the earlier kouroi, such as those from Sounion or Volomandra.

Galleries 14 and 15

The sanctuary of Aphaia on Aegina is the provenance of an interesting ensemble of sculptures (heads and arms), some of which are from the compositions on the pediments of the temple and others are fragments of *ex-votos*.

Art historians have named the period from 480 BC, that is the end of the Persian Wars until the mid-5th c.

Votive relief, of a youth crowning himself with a wreath, "Autostephanoumenos". Sounion. c. 460 BC (no. 3344).

Large votive relief, with Demeter, Persephone and Triptolemos. Eleusis. 440-430 BC (no. 126).

Zeus or Poseidon. The sea bed off Cape Artemision in Euboea. c. 460 BC (no. X 15161).

BC as that of the "Severe style". It is essentially the early phase of Classical art, preceding the creations of the great artists who worked on the most important monument of Antiquity, the Parthenon. Dominating the centre of the gallery 15 is the bronze statue of Zeus or Poseidon (no. X 15161), which was dredged up from the depths of the sea off Cape Artemision in Euboea. Dated to around 460 BC, it is thought by many scholars to be a work by the famous sculptor Kalamis. This statue is only slightly earlier than the Classical creations, since the figure's pose and movement are far removed from the strict and restrained format. The Omphalos Apollo (no. 45), a work of the 1st century AD, is a marble copy of a bronze original of c. 460 BC, which was an early work by Pheidias. Exhibited in the same Gallery is a series of funerary reliefs from various places outside Attica, since towards the end of the 6th c. BC Kleisthenes passed a law prohibiting luxurious sepulchral monuments in Athens. The stele of Amphotto (no. 739) comes from Thebes, while the votive disc from Melos with the bust of Aphrodite (no. 3990) emanates the balmy breeze of the Aegean. The votive relief no. 3344, from Sounion, with a representation of a young athlete crowning himself with a wreath (*Autostephanoumenos*) is an example of Attic sculpture in the "Severe style".

Funerary lekythos of Myrrhine. Athens. c. 420 BC (no. 4485).

Funerary stele of a young man. Salamis. 430-420 BC (no. 715).

Gallery 16

During the decade 430-420 BC, while Athens was embroiled in the Peloponnesian War, funerary stelae reappeared in the city. At first these were relatively small with one or two figures executed in low relief, whereas later they were of monumental proportions. The figures on the stelae of the last quarter of the 5th c. BC echo those of the Parthenon sculptures, such as e.g. the stele of a youth from Salamis (no. 715), which is rightly considered a work by Pheidias's famous pupil, Agorakritos. Contemporary with the funerary stelae are the monumental marble vases, lekythoi with relief representations, set up on graves. Le-

Votive relief, representing the abduction of the nymph Basile by the hero Eche-los. Phaleron in Attica. c. 410 BC (no. 1783).

Grave stele of Hegeso. The Kera-meikos. 410-400 BC (no. 3624).

kythos no. 4485, showing the deceased female Myr-rhine being led by Hermes *psychopompos* (leader of souls) to Hades is a good example.

Gallery 17

The fragments of marble metopes with represen-tations of an Amazonomachy, parts of the *sima* and a head of a marble statue of Hera are all from that goddess's temple in her sanctuary, the Heraion, at Argos and are in the tradition of the great Argeian sculptor Polykleitos. Also exhibited in this gallery are some votive reliefs that had been set up in sanctuaries as dedications by worshippers. Among the most sig-nificant are the relief with the abduction of the nymph Basile by the hero Echelos (no. 1783) and the well-known actors' relief (no. 1500) with Dionysos reclin-ing on a couch and three actors holding masks; many scholars maintain that this sculpture was dedicated after a performance of Euripides' tragedy *Bacchae*.

Gallery 18

By the late 5th and the early 4th c. BC the funerary reliefs acquired a more monumental aspect and the stele was now in the form of a small temple (*naiskos*) with antae and a pediment. Among the subjects represented the valedictory type (*dexioses*) was established, in which a relative (wife, parents) bids farewell to the dead. The figures, usually two or three, acquire a greater spiritual content with principal feature the isolation of the dead from the other figures. Outstanding is stele no. 765, with Mikka bidding her husband Dion(as) farewell, and the stele of Hegeso (no. 3624) with the dead female seated on a stool and drawing a trinket from the jewellery casket (*pyxis*) held by the maidservant standing in before her. This expressive work is thought to be by the famous sculptor in the "Rich style", Kallimachos.

The "Varvakeion Athena". A marble copy of Pheidias' chryselephantine statue of Athena Parthenos. The area of Varvakeion at Athens. c. 3rd AD (no. 129).

Galleries 19-20

With very few exceptions, the 5th c. BC statues in the round, most of them of bronze, were lost mainly in their transfer to Rome, when Greece became a province of the Roman Empire. Their beauty and fame led many sculptors to copy them in marble later. Such replicas of some of the magnificent works by major artists of the 5th c. BC are exhibited in these two galleries. Outstanding among the sculptures originally by Pheidias are the Apollo Parnopios, in a series of copies commonly known as the "Kassel Apollo", and the Athena Parthenos (no. 129), known as the "Varvakeion Athena" after its find spot. The marble statuette is the most faithful copy, on a much smaller scale, of the enormous chryselephantine statue created by Pheidias to stand in the Parthenon. Statue no. 3949 renders the type of the cult statue of the goddess Nemesis, which stood in her sanctuary at Rhamnus, created by the sculptor Agorakritos, c. 430 BC.

Galleries 21 and 34

These galleries are in fact the passage between the ground floor and upper storey of the Museum and the works exhibited in them are not in chronological order. Gallery 21 houses the *Diadoumenos*, the marble statue of the Roman period (no. 1826) which copies a famous 5th c. BC work by Polykleitos, and the bronze statue of a horse and rider ("jockey") (no. X 15177), which dominates at the centre. Recovered from the depths of the sea off Cape Artemision, it is dated in the mid-2nd c. BC. Among the works are also the Maid and the Matron of Herculaneum, Hermes of Atalante and others.
At the centre of Gallery 34 is a marble altar, while mainly votive reliefs are exhibited around it, in an attempt to give the picture of an open-air sanctuary.

Bronze statue of a horse and rider (jockey). The shipwreck off Cape Artemision. c. 140 BC (no. X 15177).

Statue of an athlete binding his hair (Diadoumenos). Marble copy, c. 100 BC, of a bronze original of the third quarter of the 5th c. BC, by the sculptor Polykleitos. Delos (no. 1826).

Statue of a Nereid or an Aura on horse-back, from the lateral acroterium of the west pediment of the temple of Asklepios at Epi-daurus. c. 380 BC (no. 157).

Gallery 22

This important ensemble of architectural sculptures decorated the temple of Asklepios at Epidaurus. According to epigraphical testimonia, four sculptors worked on the temple, among them Timotheos and Hektoridas. Represented on the east pediment was the Fall of Troy (*Iliupersis*) and on the west an Amazonomachy. Outstanding among the impressive acroteria are the female figures mounted on horseback, which are interpreted as Aurai emerging from the Ocean.

Galleries 23-24

The late 5th c. BC grave stelae quickly gave way to opulent, monumental, sepulchral works, while from the 4th c. BC the *naiskoi* were transformed

Grave stele of a youth with his father and a slave boy. A work by the school of Skopas. The Ilisos river, Athens. c. 340 BC (no. 869).

Votive relief, with representation of healing a sick man. The sanctuary of Amphiaraos at Oropos. First half of 4th c. BC (no. 3369).

into actual edicules. Imprinted on the figures, sculpted virtually in the round, in life-size or larger, are the pathos and sadness of death, as in the Ilisos stele (no. 869), which is possibly a work by the school of Skopas from Paros. The *naiskoi* of the family of Prokleides and that of Alexos from Sounion are among the most characteristic examples of large funerary monuments.

Gallery 25

Gathered here are votive reliefs from different places. The grotto-like reliefs were *ex-votos* in rural sanctuaries where the Nymphs, Pan and other minor deities were worshipped. The reliefs dedicated to Asklepios, with representations of the god and members of his family, are from the Asklepieion in Athens, on the south slope of the Acropolis.

Also displayed are some decrees with treaties between Athens and other cities or decisions to honour persons who were benefactors of the city in one way or another.

Head of Hygeia. The temple of Athena Alea at Tegea. c. 360 BC (no. 3602).

Funerary naiskos of Aristonautes. Keramei-kos. c. 310 BC (no. 738).

Gallery 28

Exhibited here are representative works of the Late Classical period (4th c. BC) which give some idea of the spirit of such great creators as Prax-iteles, Skopas, Bryaxis and Euphranor.

The latest Attic funerary monuments, such as that of Aristonautes (no. 738), date from the decade 320-310 BC. The size, the extravagant luxury and the cost of making them led Demetrios Phalireus to pass a sumptuary law in 317 BC, banning the erection of funerary monuments in the cemeteries of Athens.

The bronze ephebe from Marathon (no. X 15118) is attributed to Praxiteles or to one of his pupils while the imposing bronze statue of Paris or Perseus, from the shipwreck off Antikythera (no. X 13396), was sculpted possibly by Euphranor.

Bronze statue of an ephebe, possibly a work by the sculptor Euphranor. The shipwreck off Antikythera. 340-330 BC (no. X 13396).

Bronze statue of an ephebe, a work by Praxiteles or by one of his pupils. Marathon. 340-330 BC (no. X 15118).

Statue of Themis, a work by Chairestra-
tos. Rhamnus. 3rd c. BC (no. 231).

Statue of Poseidon. Melos. Last quarter of 2nd c. BC (no. 235).

Statue of a wounded Gaul. Delos. c. 100
BC (no. 247).

Galleries 29-30

In the closing years of the 4th c. BC, with Alexander the Great's epic conquest of the Orient and the creation of the kingdoms by his successors (*Diadochoi*), with all that entailed, the Greek spirit was enriched with a cosmopolitan content. Artists no longer worked exclusively in the major centres and sanctuaries of mainland Greece, but turned towards the periphery of the Hellenic world and particularly to the cities of the newly founded kingdoms, mainly in Asia Minor, where the rulers and the affluent merchants spared no expense in the conspicuous display of wealth and glory.

So important workshops developed in the islands and the large Hellenistic cities such as Pergamon, Alexandria, Rhodes, Ephesos and elsewhere. The sculptures of this period are distinguished by their realism, size and movement. Three centuries of creation are represented in these two galleries: from the colossal statues in the group by the Messenian sculptor Damophon, for the temple of Despoina at Lykosoura in Arcadia, and the Wounded Gaul (no. 247), from Delos, representative of the so-called "Hellenistic baroque" of the Pergamene School, to the Poseidon from Melos (no. 235) with its lordly pose, and the charming group of Aphrodite, Pan and Eros (no. 3335).

Group of Aphrodite, Pan and Eros. Delos. c. 100 BC (no. 3335).

Relief plaque with representation of the music contest between Apollo and Marsyas. Mantineia, Arcadia. 330-320 BC (no. 215).

Portrait head of a man. The Theatre of Dionysos, Athens. Late 2nd c. AD (no. 419).

Galleries 31-33

The eastwards expansion of the Roman Empire began in the 2nd c. BC with the subjugation of Macedonia and its transformation into a Roman province. All the Greek regions and the Hellenistic kingdoms were gradually conquered by the Romans, until 31 BC, the year in which the last and mightiest kingdom of the Ptolemies capitulated. Art naturally adapted to the spirit of the age, serving imperial propaganda to a considerable degree. Portrait statues and busts were the principal products of the workshops, together with relatively few idealistic works produced in the classizing periods, in the reigns of Augustus, Hadrian and the Antonines. Exhibited in Gallery 31 are works spanning the period from Augustus to Domitian, with portraits of the Julian-Claudian and Flavian dynasties, while in gallery

Bronze statue of Emperor Octavian Augustus (31 BC - AD 14). The sea bed between Aghios Efstratios and Euboea. c. 10 BC (no. X 23322).

31A are exclusively portraits of *kosmetes* (instructors in the gymnasia) and honorific stelae from the Diogeneion Gymnasium at Athens.

Gallery 32 is devoted to the 2nd c. AD with two of the best surviving portraits of Emperor Hadrian (no. 249) and his favourite Antinoos (no. 417), as well as of members of the Antonine dynasty.

Exhibited in Gallery 33 are several portraits from the reigns of the Severi, outstanding among which is the bronze statue of Julia Mamaea, mother of Alexander Severus. The tour of the Sculpture Collection concludes with the final portraits of the period of the Tetrarchy and the reign of Theodosius the Great. So the visitor forms a very good picture of the history of ancient Greek sculpture.

NIKOLAOS KALTSAS

Portrait bust of Antinoos, Emperor Hadrian's favourite. Patras. AD 130-138 (no. 417).

Bronze statuette of a woman holding a dove. Pindos. c. 460 BC (no. Kar. 540).

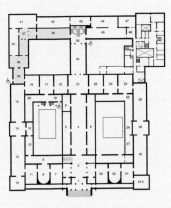

The National Archaeological Museum has one of the richest collections of ancient bronzes. It includes a few large statues, but mainly works in the minor arts, most of which were votive offerings in sanctuaries, such as the sanctuary of Zeus at Dodone, at Olympia and in the Idaean Cave on Crete; of Athena on the Acropolis at Athens; of Apollo in Boeotia (Ptoos), Phoiniki (Hyperteleatas) in Laconia and Longas (Korythos) in Messenia; of Hera at Argos and Perachora (Akraia, Limenia); of Artemis (Orthia) at Sparta, Lousoi (Hemera) in ancient Arcadia and Kalydon (Laphria) in Aetolia; of Zeus (Thaulios) and of Artemis (Enodia) at Pherai in Thessaly etc. In these works of small dimensions, many of which are masterpieces, creations of major bronzesmithing workshops, such as at Athens and in the Peloponnese (Corinth, Sicyon, Argos, Sparta *et alia*), as well as of smaller, local ones, the entire development of the art can be followed, from Geometric to Roman times. These bronzes also give an insight into the society of the ancient Greeks, facilitating understanding of diverse aspects of private and public life. The works are exhibited in Galleries 36-39.

Bronze statuette of a rider and horse. Sanctuary of Zeus at Dodone. Corinthian workshop. 575-550 BC (no. Kar. 27+X 16547).

Gallery 36

Bronze was widely used in Antiquity, in buildings, in statuary, for making and decorating various domestic and votive objects. Two techniques were mainly employed for making bronze objects: hammering, which is also the older, and casting, with which were created solid or hollow works, by the 'lost wax' (*cire perdue*) method.

Bronze figurine of a dancing ithyphallic Silen. Corinthian workshop. Sanctuary of Zeus at Dodone. Second half of 6th c. BC (no. Kar. 22).

The earliest bronzes in the collection are mainly male, female and animal figurines, rather clumsily made and schematic, characteristic of the early years of Geometric period which spans the 10th to the 8th c. BC. Many early figurines of this kind have been found in sanctuaries, along with minor works of art. In addition to the small objects, large vessels were also dedicated in sanctuaries during the 9th and 8th c. BC. These are the tripod cauldrons, frequently decorated with animal and male figures, which became increasingly sophisticated over time. The round handle with the little horse X 7842 and the warriors X 7729, X 7415 belonged to such vessels.

Finds from sanctuaries as well as from graves are numerous and varied, as borne out by the jewellery accompanying a female burial of the 8th c. BC at Dadi, Parnassis.

An abundance of bronze objects comes from the sanctuary of Zeus Naios (the epithet derives from an ancient Greek verb which means to dwell) at Dodone, where the Epirot antiquarian, politician and landowner K. Karapanos conducted excavations in 1875. Oracular inscriptions, decrees, parts of large statues, figurines of humans, deities and animals, vases and vessels, jewellery, tools, weapons, etc. were found at the site. The objects originate from various workshops, mainly Corinthian, and span a long period, from Geometric into Roman times. The figurine of a female runner Kar. 24 is most probably the creation of a Laconian workshop, whereas the ithyphallic Silen Kar. 22 comes from a Corinthian workshop. Both figurines are dated in the 6th c. BC. Many of the votive offerings to Zeus are inscribed with the name of the dedicator and of the honoured deity, such as the vase Kar. 441 and the mirror Kar. 438. A find of major historical importance is the inscribed part of shield Kar. 514, booty from the victory of King Pyrrhos of the Molossians over the Romans in 280 BC. Noteworthy among the cheek-pieces from helmets of various types is Kar. 166, of the early 4th c. BC, with an embossed representation of two men in combat. Votive offerings such as the miniature axes Kar. 173, Kar. 174, the lead jumping-weights in the form of a boar Kar. 855a,b, the goads Kar. 146-149, refer to festivals and rituals celebrated in the sanctuary. Exquisite artworks are the figurines of a horseman Kar. 27+X 16547 and of Zeus X 16546, of the 6th and the 5th c. BC respectively, as well as the *peplophoros* statuette (of a female figure wearing a heavy tunic) holding a dove (priestess or goddess) Kar. 540, of the years around 460 BC, which was discovered in the region of the Pindos mountains.

During the 8th and 7th c. BC, minor works with distinctive traits, which are known conventionally as "Macedonian bronzes", enjoyed wide diffusion, particularly in Thessaly, Macedonia, and northern areas generally. Several of their types lived on into the 6th-5th c. BC. Such objects, mainly bird-shaped pendants, bow and spectacle fibulae, as well as other minor objects, were found in large number in the sanctuary of Zeus Thaulios and of Artemis Enodia at Pherai in Thessaly. The majority date from the 8th-7th c. BC.

Outstanding among the finds from Thessalian sites are the figurines of a hoplite (foot-soldier) possibly of Achilles, X 12831, dated in the 7th c. BC, and of Athena X 11715, dated in the first half of the 6th c. BC.

Bronze statuette of Zeus holding a thunderbolt. Sanctuary of Zeus at Dodone. c. 450 BC (no. X 16546).

Bird-shaped pendant. Sanctuary of Zeus Thaulios at Pherai in Thessaly. 8th c. BC (no. X 15504).

Of impressive quantity are the animal figurines, primarily of bulls in bronze and in lead, which are the most popular *ex-votos* in the sanctuary of the Kabeiroi in Boeotia. Most are dated to the 7th and 6th c. BC and are products of local workshops.

The sanctuary of Apollo at Ptoon, also in Boeotia, is the provenance of bronze statuettes of the 6th c. BC, some bearing dedicatory inscriptions to the god (X 7380, X 7381). Bow fibulae (a kind of "safety-pin"), the pin of which was fastened in a catch-plate decorated with incised motifs, are considered as characteristic creations of Boeotian workshops and are dated mainly to the late 8th and the early 7th c. BC. They have been found as grave goods in mortuary context and as votive offerings in panhellenic and local sanctuaries, such as the fibula X 11765 from the Idaean Cave on Crete, displayed in Gallery 37.

From the important political and religious centre of the Aetolian Confederacy, Thermos, where Apollo Thermios was worshipped, come the statuette of an armed figure X 14494, which is related to Syrian works, and the warrior figurines X 14755, X 14756 of the years around

Figurine of a hoplite, possibly Achilles. Karditsa. First half of 7th c. BC (no. X 12831).

Figurine probably of Apollo. Sanctuary of Apollo at Ptoon in Boeotia. It bears inscription on the thigh: Eugeitias dedicated (it) at Ptoon. c. 510 BC (no. X 7381).

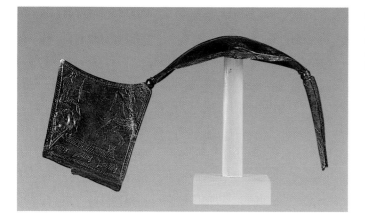

Boeotian fibula with engraved decoration of two archers. On the other side, the struggle between Herakles and Molionoi. Idaean Cave on Crete. Early 7th c. BC (no. X 11765).

700 BC. The sanctuary of Artemis Laphria at Kalydon in Aetolia is the provenance of the early 5th-c. BC small bowl 16104, with dedicatory inscription to the goddess, armbands of shields with embossed representations (X 16087, X 16088), figurines of animals, birds, etc.

Gallery 37

Significant examples of metalwork are included among the *ex-votos* recovered from sanctuaries in the Peloponnese. Although not as renowned as the great panhellenic sanctuaries, these were nevertheless important local centres where devotees offered their gifts. The offerings reflect the religious faith and the economic status of their dedicators. They are also notable works of minor sculpture, which bear witness to the traits of local yet accomplished workshops. Represented among them are artistic centres which flourished mainly in the 6th and 5th c. BC, in Corinth, Argos, Sicyon, Arcadia, Laconia and elsewhere.

A large number of *ex-votos*, mainly jewellery but also cut-out anthropomorphic and inscribed metal sheets, has been brought to light in the sanctuary of Artemis Hemera at Lousoi. The majority date from the 8th to the 6th c. BC. Contemporary with these are the finds from the sanctuary of Hera at Perachora, excellent-quality works with pronounced features of Corinthian art. Impressive is the dove figurine X 16173, which perhaps belonged to a statue of the 6th c. BC.

The votive offerings from the famous sanctuary of Asklepios at Epidaurus are associated primarily with the healing power of the god. Of interest are the in-

Dove figurine, probably from a statue. The sanctuary of Hera in Perachora. 6th c. BC (no. X 16173).

Figurine of a young man carrying a hydria (pitcher). The sanctuary of Apollo Hyperteleatas at Phoiniki in Laconia. c. 525-500 BC (no. X 7614).

scribed tablet X 8166 of Kallistratos, referring to his occupation as a cook, and the hand X 7865, holding a bleeding-cup.

There were thriving local sanctuaries in Laconia during the 6th and 5th c. BC, many of them dedicated to Apollo. From the abundant ex votos in the sanctuary of Apollo Hyperteleatas at Phoiniki, the figurine X 7614, of a young man carrying a hydria (pitcher), merits attention. From the other important sanctuary of Apollo, at Amyklai, comes the inscribed discus X 8618, weighing 3,680 grams, which had been dedicated by a victorious athlete in some games. The sanctuary of Apollo Tyritas in Kynouria is the provenance of two plastic vases X 18808 and X 18805, in the form of a horse and a Siren respectively, as well as the lion-shaped fibula X 18810 with a dedicatory inscription to the god. Finds from the sanctuary of Apollo Maleatas at Kosmas, also bear the name of the honoured god such as the figurines of a hoplite, X 7598 and a billy-goat X 7666. In the Messenian sanctuary of Apollo Korythos at Longas, Pylia, the god was worshipped as a warrior and a healer. His appellation is associated with the ancient Greek word "korys", which means helmet. From the sanctuary comes the warrior figurine X 14789, of the second half of the 6th c. BC, product of a Laconian workshop. Outstanding among the other votive offerings are weapons, some with dedicatory inscriptions, such as the spear-butts X 14818, X 14819, of the 5th c. BC, as well as their contemporary figurines of nude youths pouring libations. In the sanctuary of Pamisos at Aghios Floros, the river-god was worshipped as a healer and as protector of children, which is why a large number of the votive offerings of the 6th and 5th c. BC represent nude young figures.

Mountainous Arcadia was home to a host of sanctuaries, dedicated to deities such as Zeus, Athena, Hermes, Artemis, Pan, Demeter and Kore. One of the most revered and important cult sites was the sanctuary of Zeus on Mount Lykaion. Many of the figurines found there represent the god himself (X 13206, X 13207, X 13208). Among them, the Zeus X 13209, of 550-525 BC, is rendered in all his majesty, holding a lightning and thunder and a thunderbolt. Figurines from the rural sanctuary of Pan Nomios, protector of herds, flocks, shepherds and farmers, close to the village of Neda

(Berekla), usually represent the dedicators themselves (X 13053, X 13057, X 13059, X 13060), some of which bear the animal they offer to the god.

The miniature sheet-metal mirrors, such as X 13101/1-4, of the 6th c. BC, were *ex-votos* to the goddesses Aphrodite and Artemis, who were worshipped on Mount Kotilon, the miniature helmets X 13846/2,9,12, cuirasses X 13841/1-2, greaves X 13849/5,9 and shields X 13845/1, 20,21, were offerings in the sanctuary of Apollo Epikourios at Vassai, and were appropriate to the initially martial character of the god.

The figurine of Athena X 14828, from the sanctuary of Athena Alea at Tegea, work of the mid-6th c. BC, renders an early form of the goddess. Arcadian works are the figurines of females, such as the peplophoros (a figurine wearing a heavy tunic) X 7605, of 470 BC, and the seated goddess X 14922, of the same date, which were found in the neighbouring sanctuary of Demeter and Kore at Aghios Sostis.

Figurine of Zeus. The sanctuary of god on Mount Lykaion, in Arcadia. c. 550-525 BC (no. X 13209).

The excavations of the German Archaeological Institute in the panhellenic sanctuary of Zeus at Olympia have yielded important works of art in bronze. Most date from the 8th to the 5th c. BC. They were produced in highly-esteemed bronze workshops of Antiquity, such as the Attic, Argive, Laconian, Eleian, Ionian and others. Common *ex-votos* of the 8th and 7th c. BC at Olympia were the tripod cauldrons with figurines of nude male figures, warriors or men possibly holding reins (X 6177, X 6178, X 6179) and horses (X 6213, X 6240, X 6241) on the large round handles (X 7483), and the cauldrons with griffin protomes (X 6159, X 6160, X 6161, X 6162) and winged figures (X 6123) on the body. From the 6th c. BC, various vases and vessels were dedicated in the sanctuary of Zeus. The kore X 6149, product of a Samian workshop, will have supported a vessel of this kind. Many *ex-votos* also bore inscriptions, such as the trefoil-mouth oinochoe (wine jug) X 7948, dedicated by the Eleians to Zeus Olympios. Copious pieces of armour and weapons, both defensive (helmet, greaves, ankle-guards, foot-guards, shields etc.) and offensive (spearheads, spear-butts, swords etc.), were discovered during the excavations in the sanctuary. Votive offerings of this kind were made to the father of the gods as tokens of gratitude for military victories. The spear-butt X 6259,

Figurine of a seated goddess. The sanctuary of Demeter and Kore at Aghios Sostis, in Arcadia. 470 BC (no. X 14922).

Head of Zeus. Olympia. Late 6th c. BC (no. X 6440).

Statuette of Athena Promachos, dedicated by Meleso. The Acropolis at Athens. 480-470 BC (no. X 6447).

of the years 443-433 BC, *ex-voto* of the Tarantines from the booty of the Thourians, is a case in point. As is to be expected, the *ex-votos* included statuettes of Zeus: the earlier ones in the type of the god "in epiphany" (X 6093, X 6098, X 6108, X 6167, X 6168, of the 8th c. BC), the later ones as the guardian of divine order, with thunderbolt (X 6194, X 6195, X 6196, of 500-450 BC). Exquisite works of art are the head X 6440 and the statuette of the god X 6163, of the late 6th c. BC.

Equally important are the finds from the excavations of the Archaeological Society at Athens in the sanctuary of Athena on the Acropolis of Athens. The tripod cauldrons were the most popular votive offerings during the 8th and 7th c. BC as at Olympia. Figurines of nude males (X 6617, X 6618, X 6734), men possibly holding reins (X 6593), warriors (X 6612, X 6613, X 6616, X 6620) and horses (X 6539, X 6541, X 6544, X 6697) once adorned the handles, the rim or the body of such vessels. The griffin protomes (X 6633, X 6635, X 6636, X 6639) decorated the body of the cauldrons of the 7th c. BC. Various vases and vessels were commonly dedicated to Athena. From most only the cast parts have survived, such as the inscribed handles of basins (X 7175, X 7178, X 17529) and their tripod stands with legs imitating those of lions or horses (X 7023). Of superb art are the handles of basin-like vessels X 6647 decorated with lions rending a deer, and X 7128 with lizards, both of the late 6th c. BC. Female figures in multi-pleated garments, as well as male ones in lively movement, ornamented various vases of the 6th and 5th c. BC (X 6474, X 6476, X 6477, X 6479). The figure of a youth mounted on a dolphin X 6626, a work of the years around the mid-5th c. BC, once graced a large vessel. Among the utilitarian objects from domestic life were the lamps. One of these, X 7038, of the late 5th c. BC, is in the form of a ship and bears an inscription denoting that it was dedicated to Athena. Female statuettes of the late 6th and the early 5th c. BC represent the patron goddess herself. On most of them Athena is rendered in the type of the Promachos, with shield and spear. The largest of these, X 6447, of 480-470 BC, is inscribed with the name of the female dedicator, Meleso. In addition to figures of Athena, the *ex-votos* include a large number of statuettes of secular figures, such as kouroi, korai, rustics, shepherds, athletes. The head X 6590 possibly belonged to a statuette of an athlete. Life-size statues also stood in the sanctuary on the Acropolis. Fragments of some of these have survived, such as the early 5th-c. BC head of a bearded warrior X 6446. A host of weapons was also dedicated to the goddess. Particularly interesting are the inscribed spear-butts X 6843, X 6844, X 6849, X 11455 and X 6869, as well as parts of the arm-bands and interior straps of shields with embossed representations (X 6958, X 6961, X 6964, X 6965, X 6967). Among the *ex-votos* which come from island sanctuaries the North Syrian blinker X 15070, of the 9th c. BC, from the sanctuary of Apollo Daphnephoros in Eretria on Euboea, is especially fascinating because it attests to relations and contacts with different peoples. It bears a representation of a "Master of Animals" and an Aramaic inscription. The late 7th-c. BC fountain-spout X 16512, in the form of a lion head with frog, from the sanctuary of Hera (Heraion) on Samos, is an original Samian work. This sanctuary is also the provenance of the statuette of a flute-player X 16513, dated to the years around 550-525 BC. Visible on the head are the "phorbeia", the straps, which held the flute in place in the mouth.

A plethora of votive offering has been recovered from the Idaean Cave on Crete, where, myth has it, Zeus was born and brought up. These include vases, animal figurines, parts of shields with embossed representations, jewellery, objects of ivory and gold, many of which are imports from the Orient and Egypt. Most of the finds date to the late 8th-early 7th c. BC, when the sanctuary enjoyed a heyday.

Fountain-spout in the form of a lion-head topped by a frog. Heraion on Samos. Late 7th c. BC (no. X 16512).

Gallery 38

Medical instruments of different types and uses point to the development of the science of Medicine in Antiquity and to its widespread application.

Various kinds of musical instruments emphasize the high regard in which man held music and dance. The sounds from string (lyre X 15104), percussion (cymbals X 7958β, X 7959, sistrum X 7840) and wind (flutes A3768, Kar. 668) instruments accompanied all manner of occasions in public and private life.

The objects used on the door and couch models, the lamp

Bronze lyre. The shipwreck off Anti-kythera. Hellenistic period (no. X 15104).

stands X 13164, X 14486 and the incense-burner X 7439, provide information about the house and daily life. Vases both domestic and ritual, gaming pieces (die X 7515, knuckle-bone X 18844), as well as tools and implements were used for everyday tasks and activities.

Essential accessories of the female toilet were the mirrors. Whether with a handle-support, hand mirrors or folding ones, these were widely diffused. They are products of accomplished toreutic workshops of the 6th-3rd c. BC, and are embellished with diverse decorative motifs.

Bronze mirror. Athens. c. 455 BC (no. X 7579).

Hydrias were large vases used mainly for carrying liquids but also as cinerary urns and prizes to victors in contests. Most of them date from the 6th to the 4th c. BC and are creations of famous bronze workshops, mainly of Attica and Corinth.

The mechanism X 15087, one of the most significant and intriguing scientific instruments of Antiquity, dated around 80 BC, was found in 1901 in an ancient shipwreck on the seabed off the island of Antikythera, along with other superb antiquities, such as the statues of the Ephebe X 13396 in Gallery 28 and the Philosopher X 14300 in Gallery 29. The mechanism was used for astronomical and calendrical calculations and consists of a complex system of gear wheels and plaques bearing inscriptions and planetary indications. From the same shipwreck comes a host of marble sculptures (in the Museum Atrium) as well as bronze statuettes (X 13397, X 13398, X 13399, X 15110). Equally interesting is the hand X 15111, which would belonged to a larger than life-size statue of a boxer. The majority of the bronze statuettes are creations of the 2nd c. BC, which display overt influences from works of the 5th and 4th c. BC.

The statuette of Dionysos X 15209, from the region of Eurytania, is also dated in the 2nd c. BC.

In 1964, in the neighbourhood of Ambelokipoi in Athens, Roman bronze statues were brought to light. Most of the bronzes are copies in miniature or remodellings of well-known works of the Classical and Hellenistic periods. Among them, the Discobolus (Discus-thrower) X 16781 is a copy of the renowned work by Myron, while figure X 16785 is rendered in the type of the Doryphoros (Spear-bearer) by the Argive sculptor Polykleitos.

Gallery 39

From the field of the battle of Thermopylai, where the Greeks fought a heroic battle against the Persians in 480 BC, comes a large number of bronze and iron arrowheads.

Exhibited here is the reconstruction of a bronze chariot (Kar. 780-794) of the 3rd-4th c. AD, parts of which were found in the ruins of a house in Nicomedeia, in the Asia Minor province of Bithynia, as well as parts of a harness.

ROSA PROSKYNITOPOULOU

Statuette of a Discus-thrower, Roman copy of the well-known work by Myron, created c. 450 BC. Ambelokipoi in Athens (no. X 16781).

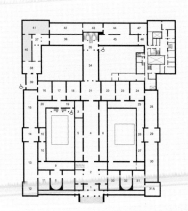

The civilization of ancient Egypt developed in the fertile valley of the river Nile. Its theocratic and polytheistic character, combined with the Egyptians' belief in life after death, determined the nature of its art and architecture. There are notable examples of its material culture in the Egyptian Collection of the National Archaeological Museum, which was formed mainly from the private collections of two expatriate Greeks living in Egypt, Ioannis Demetriou from Alexandria and Alexandros Rostovitz from Cairo, donated by them to the Museum in 1880 and 1904 respectively. The Collection is of considerable international standing, on account of the importance and rarity of its objects, representative specimens of which are exhibited in two galleries, 40-41. The pieces are presented in chronological order and cover the entire spectrum of Egyptian civilization, from early Predynastic times (5000 BC) into the Roman Age (30 BC - AD 395), and represent all aspects of art: statues, reliefs, stelae, vases, sarcophagi, mummies, Fayum portraits, minor objects, jewellery.

Exhibited in Cases VIII, IX, X, XIII and XIV, either side of the entrance to Gallery 41, are artefacts from the Prehistoric-Predynastic period.

Sycamore wood model of a boat and its crew (l. 1.35 m). A reference to the sacred pilgrimage of the dead to Abydos, burial place and cult centre of Osiris. Middle Kingdom, 12th Dynasty, 1994-1782 BC (Case XVI, no. Ξ221).

Predynastic period (5000-3100 BC)

This covers the Neolithic and Chalcolithic periods, when several cultural centres developed in the southern (Upper Egypt) and the northern (Lower Egypt) parts of the Nile valley. The most important of these were in Upper Egypt. Characteristic artefacts of the Predynastic period are the stone tools and weapons (Case VIII), outstanding among which are the disc-shaped mace-head (Case VIII, no. Λ143) and the cosmetic palettes (Case IX). The latter are stone vessels used originally for pulverizing the mineral malachite and mixing it with water: the paste was used as make-up round the eyes, in order to protect them from the sun's rays. The palettes evolved from simple disc and trapezoidal shape to cut-out shapes of animals and birds, and acquired a ceremonial use. The stone vases nos 1791, Λ173, Λ180 (Case XIII), of unrivalled workmanship and beauty, were for funerary use. Noteworthy too are the clay vases nos 6882α, β, 6889, 6890, AK 34 (Case XIII) and 6884α-δ (Case XIV), and lastly, the jewellery, particularly the ivory pieces Δ185-Δ195 (Case X) which came from child burials.

Early Dynastic period (3100-2650 BC. 1st-2nd Dynasty)

This is the beginning of the historical period, during which the foundations of Egyptian civilization were laid, with the evolution and unification of the pre-existing cultures in the Nile valley. A strong central authority was established with paramount ruler the pharaoh, King of Upper and Lower Egypt, and a class of nobles. Hieroglyphic script developed and advances were made in the arts and crafts, the roots of which lie in the Predynastic tradition. This can be seen in stone vases nos Λ185-Λ187 (Cases V and VI) and the cosmetic palettes, which became larger and were transformed into royal votive objects (Case X, no. Λ22). The major achievement of Early Dynastic art is sculpture, which is distinguished by naturalism and monumentality (Case I, no. 13, and Case X, nos 832, 759). The statues of pharaohs, humans and sacred animals (hippopotamus, baboon), in both stone and ivory, are smaller than life-size and represent heavy figures, standing, sitting or squatting, with large head and in strictly frontal pose.

Early hippopotamus statue in granite (l. 0.45 m). The body is schematically rendered in contrast to the naturalistically worked head. Early Dynastic period, c. 3000 BC (Case I, no. 13).

Rose granite statue of the royal scribe Rahotep (h. 0.735 m). Old Kingdom, 5th Dynasty, 2465-2350 BC (Case XII, no. 11).

Old Kingdom (2650-2155 BC. 3rd-6th Dynasty)

A period of prosperity and powerful pharaohs who, when sun worship was established as the official religion of the state (5th Dynasty), were addressed as Sons of Ra. A golder age in architecture and sculpture, in which ambitious artistic projects were realized. The pyramids were established as the tombs of the pharaohs and the mastabas (rectangular constructions) as those of members of the royal family and of nobles. From the cult chamber of the mastaba come the false-doors – depictions of doors on stone stelae – which mark the place where offerings are made to the spirit (Ka) of the deceased (Case II, nos 28, 30). Most of the Old Kingdom sculptures come from tombs. Their basic features are absolute frontality and symmetry (Case III). Youthful male and female figures, serene and majestic, are represented in life-size, either standing – the men with the left leg to the fore, the women with the feet close together – or sitting (Case XI). In many cases they are supported by an integral pillar (Case XI, no. 24). New types were created such as the squatting scribe (Case XII, no. 11), statuettes and figurines of servants in various occupations (Cases XV and VI, Ξ219), which are carved from limestone or sycamore wood coated with stucco and painted in vivid colours.

Middle Kingdom (2134-1650 BC. 11th-13th Dynasty)

A period of wealth and of competent pharaohs (11th-12th Dynasty) who conquered Nubia to the south of Egypt, reinforced the frontiers with garrisons, exercised strong influence in the Middle East and developed trade with lands in Africa and the Eastern Mediterranean. There was a burgeoning of literature and the visual arts are characterized by a combination of technical excellence and eclecticism, resulting from the enrichment of the artistic tradition of Memphis (Old Kingdom) with new elements. Typical creations are the votive statues of private individuals, showing courtiers in robes, mature men in tunics (Case XVIII, no. Λ31) or kilts tied high on the waist (Case XVIII, nos 2066, Λ32). During the 12th-13th Dynasty it became the custom to set up – outside the tombs and inside the small

shrines in the necropolis at Abydos – rectangular, limestone, relief stelae, sometimes with semicircular finial (Case XVII). Characteristic offerings from the 12th-dynasty graves are wooden models of scenes from everyday life (Case IV, no. Ξ223), and of boats (Case XVI).

New Kingdom (1550-1070 BC. 18th-20th Dynasty)

The richest and most impressive period when Egypt, thanks to its internal stability, its regaining of control of Nubia and Libya and conquest of many small states in the Near East, became the most powerful realm in the Mediterranean. Contacts with foreign peoples and the inflow of wealth contributed to a new floruit in art and architecture. Rock-cut tombs were built on the west bank of the Nile in the city of Thebes, the famous Valley of the Kings, with separate funerary temples, as well as splendid new palaces and magnificent temples for the gods (Luxor, Karnak on the east bank of Thebes), that were adorned with imposing statues (Case XXXVI). At first art was characterized by influences from the Middle Kingdom (Cases XXXVII, XXXVIII) and the creation of new statue types, such as the stela bearer – statuette of a kneeling worshipper with a stele in front inscribed with a prayer to the sun-god Ra-Atum (Case XXV) – and later by the prevailing of new naturalistic trends that began in the reign of Amenhotep III (Case XXIV, no. 1798) and culminated and ceased in the reign of Akhenaten (Amarna style). The reign of Pharaoh Ramses II was a golden age for art and architecture, when there was conscious return to the traditional style (Case XXX, no. Λ36).

Fragment of a faience double-relief tablet with sunken relief representation of Pharaoh Amenhotep III, making an offering to the god Ptah (h. 0.145 m). New Kingdom, 18th Dynasty, 1402-1364 BC (Case XXIV, no. 1798).

Solid bronze kneeling statuette of Pharaoh Shabaka (h. 0.155 m), one of the rare representations of him. Late period, 25th Dynasty, c. 700 BC (Case XLII, no. 632).

Third Intermediate period (1070-712 BC. 21st-24th Dynasty)

A period of political weakness (21st Dynasty) and Libyan domination (22nd-24th Dynasty). The burial customs were particularly elaborate, embalming was perfected and so was metalworking. The abolition of decoration in the mortuary temples resulted in the transfer of scenes to sarcophagi, wooden funerary stelae (Case XLIV, nos Ξ198-Ξ200) and funerary papyri. A

Bronze statue of the standing princess-priestess Takusit (h. 0.69 m). Engraved decoration on the garment, inlaid with an alloy of gold and silver. Late period, 25th Dynasty, c. 715 BC (Case XLVIII, no. 110).

typical coffin of this period is wooden, anthropoid and covered with lavish painted decoration on a yellow ground (Case LXV). In the reign of Pharaoh Osorkon (22nd Dynasty) this was replaced by a new type, of cartonnage, in which the mummy case consists of layers of linen coated with stucco and painted with rich decoration (Case LIX).

Late period (712-332 BC. 25th-31st Dynasty)

In the political domain there was an alternation of foreign rulers, of Ethiopian (25th) and Persian (27th, 31st) Dynasties, with Egyptian ones (26th, Saite period, 28th-30th Dynasty). In art a tendency to revive the models of earlier periods held sway, while there was also a prolific production of bronze votive statuettes of deities (Case LIII). Characteristic are the bronze royal statues and the statuettes of the Ethiopian period, distinguished by their heavy, severe figures (Case XLII, no. 632, Case XLVIII). Usual funerary statuettes are wooden figurines of the triadic god Ptah-Socar-Osiris (Case XXXIV).

Ptolemaic period (332-30 BC)

After the conquest of Egypt by Alexander the Great (332 BC) and his sudden death, Ptolemy, son of Lagos was appointed governor of the land. He subsequently created the Hellenistic kingdom of Egypt and founded the Ptolemaic dynasty. The Ptolemies exercised an assertive domestic and foreign policy, and fostered a climate of intellectual freedom in culture. There was parallel development of Egyptian (Case LIV) and Hellenistic art, as well as the creation of a mixed style (Case XLI, no. 3355, Cases LVI, LVII, LXVIII). In the burial customs the generalized use of decoration of the linen shroud with four to six polychrome sections of cartonnage, among them the gilded face mask, held sway (Case LX).

Female portrait painted in encaustic technique on wood (h. 0.36 m). Fayum. Early Antonine period, c. AD 138-161 (Case LVIII, no. 1628).

Roman period (30 BC-AD 395)

Under Emperor Augustus Egypt became a Roman province and was the granary of Rome. With the gradual decimation of the local aristocracy the custom of placing votive statues in the temples ceased, after a period of their gradual degeneration (Case LV) and the restriction of art to the minor arts, with the splendid exception of the famous Fayum portraits (Case LVIII, nos 1627-1629).

ELENI TOURNA

Attic white lekythos. A dead warrior seated on a grave. By the Group R. Eretria. c. 410 BC (no. 1816).

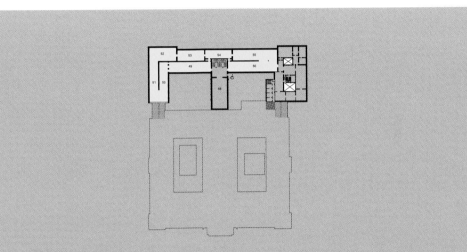

Galleries 49-56 on the first floor of the Museum are devoted to the Collection of Vases and Minor Objects. A few outstanding works, such as the monumental Geometric krater from the Dipylon no. 804, the hydria from Analatos no. 313, the Cycladic pithos-amphora no. 911, the skyphoid krater of Prometheus no. 16384, the red-figure kylix no. 1666, gift of Ch. Trikoupis (former Prime Minister of Greece), the stamnos of Polygnotos no. 18063 and the pinax of Ninnion no. 11036 are exhibited in the Sculpture Galleries 7, 11, 13 and 15 for reasons of comparison.

The quantity and quality of the vases of the Geometric period, of the early black-figure vases from Vari, of the white lekythoi and of the red-figure vases of the 4th c. BC place the collection among the richest in the world.

The exhibits come from excavations mainly in cemeteries, such as the Kerameikos and at Vari, and in sanctuaries, such as those of Hera in Argos and at Perachora, of Artemis Orthia in Sparta, of the Acropolis of Athens, of the Kabeiroi in Thebes, or are fortuitous finds and gifts.

Their presentation in chronological sequence follows the development of Greek pottery from the 11th into the 4th c. BC.

Galleries 49-50

The exhibition commences, by way of introduction, with a selection of clay objects and sherds which illustrate the making and decorating of vases (Cases 1-2). Displayed in the first two galleries are vases of the Protogeometric and the Geometric period (1100-700 BC), which owes its name to the geometric motifs that encircle the vase in strictly structured zones. In the early centuries (11th-10th c. BC), in contrast to the more naturalistic motifs of Minoan and Mycenaean times, simple decorative designs appear, such as concentric circles and semicircles, zigzags, chequer-pattern, lozenges and triangles. Subsequently, in the 9th c. BC, more composite motifs appear, such as meanders, cruciform and leaf-shaped, while in the

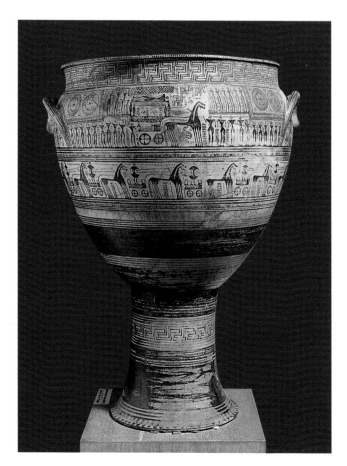

Attic Geometric krater. By the Hirschfeld Painter. The Dipylon. 750-735 BC (no. 990).

8th c. BC the human figure is established in various representations, such as sea battles, duels, hunting and, primarily the "prothesis" (lying in state) and the "ekphora" (carrying out of the body) of the dead, and the chariot races held in his honour. The Geometric style, a panhellenic phenomenon, attained its perfection in Attica and Attic vases are presented in Gallery 49. In Case 4 are finds from the Protogeometric cemetery at Nea Ionia, while in Case 5 are the burials from the so-called "Areopagos cemetery". Striking in Case 7 are the many and varied grave goods from the Middle Geometric "Isis" tomb at Eleusis, while in Cases 12, 13, 14 are Late Geometric vases from the excavations in the Kerameikos. At the far end of and dominating the gallery is the monumental funerary amphora by the Dipylon Painter, no. 803, with a scene of the ekphora of the dead.

The Analatos hydria. By the Analatos Painter. Analatos. c. 700 BC (no. 313).

Boeotian pithos-amphora. Thebes. 680-670 BC (no. 220).

Gallery 50

Apart from a small selection of vases from Attic workshops, outstanding among which, for its size and shape, is the famous Late Geometric krater by the Hirschfeld Painter, no. 990, with representation of ekphora and chariot race in honour of the dead, pottery from various provincial workshops is presented here: in Case 20 from Boeotia, Case 21 from Achaia, Argos and Laconia, Case 23 from Thessaly, Case 24 from the Aegean Islands and Case 25 from Cyprus. Displayed on pedestals are the Boeotian pithos-amphora with the unique depiction of the Mistress of Animals ("Potnia Theron") (no. 220) as well as the large amphorae nos 892, 893, 824, 11707 from Thera (mod. Santorini).
Around the late 8th c. BC, a change took place in the decorative repertoire of vases. The strict discipline and symmetry which had hitherto prevailed began to wane. Moreover, contacts with other cultures, outside Greece such as Egypt and, primarily, the near East, during the 8th c. BC, influenced artists. The thematic repertoire was renewed with depictions of wild beasts, floral ornaments and fantastical creations, forgotten for centuries. This period is called "Orientalizing" and held sway in Greek lands from about 700 to 630 BC. Pioneers in these innovations were the Corinthian

artists, who, employing new techniques and thematic repertoire, created the so-called "Protocorinthian" style (720-630 BC), examples of which can be seen in Case 22. They were the first to use the outline technique and the first to invent the black-figure style, circa 690 BC, by painting representations in black glaze, incising the outlines and details, and using added colours, white and purple.

Gallery 51

During the Orientalizing period, Attic painters created what is conventionally named the Protoattic style. Under the influence of their Corinthian colleagues, as well as of the contemporary island workshops, they experimented – hesitantly at first – and gradually advanced, applying their own techniques. They used the old technique of silhouette combined with the recent one of outline, more rarely incision, and added colour, white and purple, arriving at the polychromy which heralds the black-figure style. One of the loveliest and earliest examples of the Protoattic style is the hydria from Analatos, no. 313, in which the old elements, grazing horses in the lower part of the vase, and the new, the heraldic lions within a densely vegetated landscape, coexist (ground floor, Gallery 7 Sculptures). The amphora from Kynosarges no. 14497, with the pierced handles, continuing the tradition of the large funerary amphorae, imposes by virtue of its size and surprises with its polychromy, which enlivens the subjects of its decoration.

The large kraters in Case 29, exceptional products of the Parian workshop, are decorated with mythological scenes, such as the departure of Herakles (no. 354). Close to them, the Eretrian amphorae (Case 31), typical products of a local workshop, with representations of gods, sphinxes and lions, are striking in the simplicity of rendering the basic subjects, as well as the richness of the filling ornaments.

By the final decades of the 7th c. BC, the black figure-style, in which the representation is depicted in silhouette against the red or buff ground of the vase, with details picked out by incision and added white or purple, had prevailed. Among the most representative vases of this period are the early black-figure ones from the Anagyrous tumuli at Vari, which are displayed in

Large Cycladic pithos-amphora. Provenance unknown. c. 640 BC (no. 911).

Cases 33-40 and on pedestals. Principal painters are the Bellerophon Painter (no. 16391) and the Nessos Painter. To the latter are ascribed the skyphoid krater with depiction of Prometheus Bound (no. 16384, in Sculpture Gallery 11) and the monumental amphora with representation of Herakles overcoming the Centaur Nessos, on the neck of the vase, and the three enormous Gorgons on its body (no. 1002), which are considered among the finest works of the period.

Early Attic black-figure amphora. The struggle between Herakles and the Centaur Nessos. By the Nessos Painter. Athens. 615-605 BC (no. 1002).

Gallery 52

Exhibited in the first section of the gallery is Attic black-figure pottery (Cases 42-45) of the early 6th c. BC, with representative works by the vase-painter Sophilos and the Komasts Group, as well as pottery from the contemporary Boeotian (Cases 47-48) and Corinthian workshops (Cases 46 and 50). Dominant too in this gallery are the finds from the major sanctuaries, such as the Heraion of Argos (Cases 51 and 57, no. 15471), the Heraion at Perachora (Cases 52, 53 and 58), the sanctuary of Artemis Orthia in Sparta (Case 54) and the sacred precincts (temene) of Athena and of Poseidon at Sounion (Case 55). The votive offerings of the worshippers from these sanctuaries are many and varied, some precious, others humble: terracotta figurines and clay vases, frequently miniature, bronze models, etc. Outstanding are the ivory relief plaques from the sanctuary of Artemis Orthia and the seals from the Heraion at Perachora. Displayed in Case 56 are wooden pinakes found in the sanctuary of the Nymphs in the Pitsas Cave in the region of Corinth (no. 16464). Works of Corinthian artists, they are decorated in tempera technique and echo contemporary monumental painting. From the Archaic temple of Apollo at Thermos in Aetolia come the large terracotta metopes painted with mythological subjects.

Attic black-figure krater. The struggle between Herakles and Nereus. By the vase-painter Sophilos. Provenance unknown. c. 590 BC (no. 12587).

Terracotta house model. Heraion of Argos. 700-675 BC (no. 15471).

Wooden pinax. A sacrificial procession. Pitsas Cave, near Corinth. 540-530 BC (no. 16464).

Fragments of an Attic black-figure cantharos. Achilles is harnessing his steed. By Nearchos. Acropolis at Athens. c. 560 BC (no. 15166).

Gallery 53

In Attica in the 6th c. BC major artists whose works began to flood the foreign markets came to the fore, gradually ousting the Corinthians. Vase-painters such as Kleitias, Lydos, Nearchos, the Amasis Painter and Exekias created unique masterpieces. Presented in Case 65 is a selection of fragments of some of the most beautiful Attic black-figure vases of the 6th c. BC, which were *ex-votos* in the sanctuary of Athena on the Acropolis and were found in the Persian destruction level of 480 BC. The splendid black-figure kalyx-krater no. 26746, with representation of a battle between Greeks and Trojans around the slain Patroklos (Case 69), obviously comes from the workshop of the great vase-painter Exekias, as do the funerary plaques with scene of lamentation (threnos) nos 2414-2417 (Case 68). Impressive in Case 70 are the Euboean nuptial lebetes, for their size and representations, and in Case 72 the vases of the Middle and Late Corinthian periods, for the details of their designs.

Noteworthy are the black vases of Etruria, which imitate metal prototypes (Case 73). Among the finds from the sanctuary of Hephaisteia on Lemnos outstanding are the cut-out Sirens and the models of fountains (Case 74). From Klazomenai in Asia Minor come the clay sarcophagi with painted representations, typical examples of an Ionian workshop. Vases from Ionian workshops are also exhibited in Case 75.

Attic black-figure dinos. A Homeric battle. By the Painter of Acropolis 606. Acropolis at Athens. 570-560 BC (no. Acr. 606).

Attic black-figure lekythos. Herakles and Atlas. By the Athena Painter. Provenance unknown. Early 5th c. BC (no. 1132).

Gallery 54

The black-figure style attained its zenith circa 530 BC. Incision and added colours were no longer sufficient complementary techniques for the needs of a more naturalistic rendering of the human body or the drapery of garments. So, around that time, in a workshop in the Athenian Kerameikos, the red-figure style was created, which is the reverse of the black-figure. The ground is now painted black, leaving the figures reserved in the colour of the clay, and the details are added with a fine brush. The establishment of the red-figure style did not result in the disappearance of the black-figure, which continued alongside it until circa 480 BC. In fact, in certain cases, such as the Panathenaic amphorae and the Kabeiric vases, it remained in use for religious reasons even into Hellenistic times.

In the closing years of the 6th c. BC, eponymous vase-painters, such as Euphronios, Phintias, Smikros and others, produced innovative works of superb quality and elegance. Exhibited in Gallery 54 is black-figure and red-figure pottery representative of the late 6th and the early 5th c. BC. Among the most important pieces are the *ex-votos* found in the Persian destruction level of 480 BC on the Acropolis (Cases 86-87). Noteworthy are the large red-figure kylix by Euphronios, with scene of the wedding of Peleus and Thetis no. 15214 (Case 88), the red-figure kalyx-krater by the Berlin Painter no. Acr. 742 (Case 92) and the red-fig-

*Attic red-figure kylix. Herakles and
Dionysos. By the vase-painter Douris.
Provenance unknown. c. 470 BC
(no. 27523).*

ure kalyx-krater by the Syriskos Painter no. Acr. 735, depicting the struggle of Theseus with the Minotaur
which is exhibited in the ground floor Gallery 15,
alongside the sculptures. Striking in Case 90, for the
delicacy and refinement of its drawing, is the large red-
figure kylix no. 27523 by the painter Douris, with representation of the symposium of Herakles and
Dionysos. Also by the same artist is the charming ary-
ballos no. 15375, with Erotes chasing a youth.

*Attic red-figure kylix. A hoplite. By
the potter Phintias. Tanagra. 505-
500 BC (no. 1628).*

Attic white lekythos. Bidding a warrior farewell. By the Achilles Painter. Eretria. 450-440 BC (no. 1818).

Attic white lekythos. The visit to a tomb. By the Bosanquet Painter. Eretria. 450-440 BC (no. 1935).

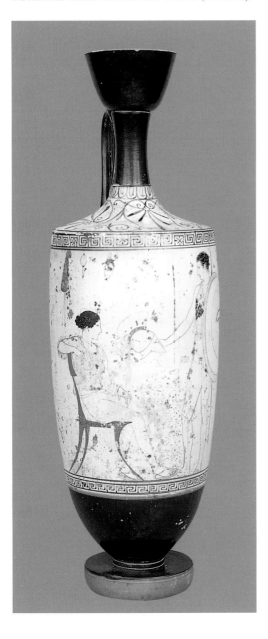

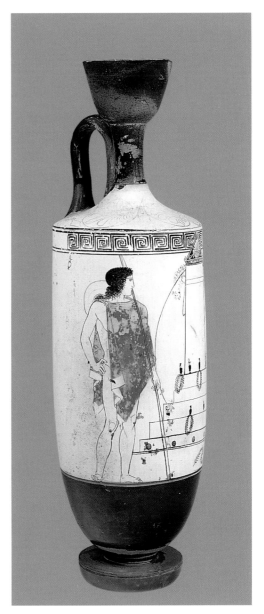

Attic white-ground kylix. The death of Orpheus. By the Pistoxenos Painter. Acropolis at Athens. 470-460 BC (no. 15190, Acr. 439).

Gallery 55

Displayed in Gallery 55 is the collection of white lekythoi, the most representative of which are by the Achilles Painter, the Sabouroff Painter and the Bosanquet Painter (Cases 109, 110). The subjects featured on these vases, such as the preparation for and the visit to the tomb, Charon, Hypnos and Thanatos, the valediction of the warrior or the prothesis of the dead, are linked directly with their mortuary use. The figures, which are rightly considered the loveliest in Attic vase-painting, emanate modesty and restrained grief.

Distinguished among the red-figure vases of the Early Classical period, and displayed in separate cases, are the pelike by the Pan Painter, with the myth of Herakles and the King of Egypt Busiris no. 9683 (Case 105) and the loutrophoros with the prothesis of the dead no. 1170 (Case 108).

At the far end of the gallery, in Cases 115-117, is an assemblage of vases, figurines and other objects associated with the life of the woman. Outstanding are the nuptial lebetes and the loutrophoroi (Case 116), while the famous epinetron (vase used in processing wool) by the Eretria Painter no. 1629, with the young bride Alkestes leaning on the bed and observing her girl friends, is placed in a special showcase (Case 118).

Attic red-figure pelike. Herakles and Busiris. By the Pan Painter. Thespies. c. 470 BC (no. 9683).

Attic red-figure epinetron. The young bride Alkestes and her girl friends. By the Eretria Painter. Eretria. c. 425 BC (no. 1629).

Attic red-figure kalyx-krater. Erotostasia (weighing of Eros and Anteros). By the Erotostasia Painter. Provenance unknown. c. 330 BC (no. 12544).

Panathenaic amphora. Eretria. 360/359 BC, during the archonship of Kallimedes (no. 20046).

Gallery 56

At the front of the gallery are Attic red-figure vases of the late 5th and the early 4th c. BC. Outstanding are those by the Eretria Painter and the Meidias Painter, representative examples of the Ornate Style. The bold innovations, such as perspective abbreviations and the use of different planes, which are observed on the red-figure pelike no. 1333 by the Pronomos Painter, with representation of Gigantomachy, reflect the influence of monumental painting (Case 123). Small plastic vases delight with their subjects and polychromy (Case 132).

The collection of red-figure vases of the 4th c. BC, is also very important, with representative works by the Erbach Painter (Case 127), the Marsyas Painter (Case 133) and the Erotostasia Painter (Case 136), as their painters have been named conventionally. Predominant shapes in this period are the kalyx-krater and the bell-krater, which are usually decorated with symposium scenes, assemblies of gods, mythological battles and, paramount, Dionysos and his entourage (thiasos). Among the most imposing vases of the 4th c. BC, the Panathenaic amphorae from Eretria, prizes awarded to the victors in the Panathenaia Games, are works by well-known red-figure vase-painters who follow the tradition of black-figure technique (Cases 130, 131). The red-figure pyxis no. 1635 with representation of Leto in childbirth, and the pelike no. 1718, with a representation of the Epaulia, the celebration on the day after the wedding (Case 135), are typical examples of the Kertch Style, as its is called conventionally after the city of Kertch, ancient Pantikapaion, in the eastern Crimea, where

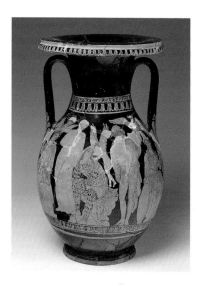

Attic red-figure pelike. The Judgement of Paris. By the Marsyas Painter. The Kerameikos. 340-330 BC (no. 1181).

many of these Late Classical vases were found. Principal traits of this style are polychromy, gilding and the penchant for detailed decoration.

In the second part of the Gallery is red-figure pottery from various provincial workshops with distinctive local styles, such as the Corinthian (Case 138), the Laconian (Cases 139, 140) and the Boeotian (Case 141). The Kabeiric vases, from the sanctuary of the Kabeiroi (Kabeirion) in Boeotia, constitute a special group (Case 142). Their main features are the black-figure technique, the humoristic disposition and the vitality distinctive of the representations, as for example on skyphos no. 424 with the parody of a rural procession.

At the far end of the room, the exhibition closes with two large units devoted to the world of children and to athletics.

ELISAVET STASINOPOULOU

Plastic vase. Protome of Aphrodite "ana-dyomene". Tanagra. Early 4th c. BC (no. 2060).

Kabeiric skyphos. Procession towards the sanctuary of the Kabeiroi. By the Mystai Painter. Thebes. Late 5th/early 4th c. BC (no. 424).

The rich and famous Stathatos Collection, donated by Heleni Stathatou in her lifetime, comprises some 970 works dating from the Bronze Age (2300 BC) to Post Byzantine period. The objects, mainly examples of the minor arts, of various materials – with special emphasis on gold jewellery of all periods –, are products of different workshops in the islands, the great cities in Asia Minor and mainland Greece as well as the East. In the exhibition an attempt is made to present this diverse material in chronological sequence, with the exception of the neck of the giant volute-krater, the bronze cauldron and the Illyrian helmet with the gold visor, which flank the entrance to the gallery.

Gold belt. From the so-called Karpenisi Hoard. 2nd c. BC (no. St. 362).

Gold hearnet. From the so-called Karpenisi Hoard. 230-220 BC (no. St. 369).

Gold earrings with the Potnia Theron (Mistress of Animals). Argos. 650-625 BC (no. St. 309).

Gallery 42

Outstanding pieces from the 3rd and 2nd millennia BC are the Minoan stone vases (Case 1) and the Mycenaean jewellery and figurines (Cases 2, 3). Characteristic Geometric and Archaic vases, terracotta figurines, bronze minor objects and jewellery (Cases 4, 5) span the 9th, 8th and 7th c. BC. The gold daedalic earrings and plaquettes are among the finest of their kind (Case 5). The Classical period is represented by significant bronzes, terracotta figurines, select gold necklaces and other jewellery from various workshops (Cases 13, 14, 15). The rich collection of early clay vases, bronze, gold and silver jewellery of the 6th, 5th and 4th c. BC, from the Chalkidiki, are displayed in three cases (Cases 9, 10, 11). An im-

Hermes carrying a ram (Kriophoros). Peloponnesian workshop. Third quarter of 6th c. BC (no. St. 328).

portant ensemble of silver vessels from Sinope includes characteristic works of Asia Minor, silver-
smithing of the Achaemenid period, early 5th c. BC
(Case 18). The Attic clay *öon* (egg model) exhibited
in the Case 19 is a rare example with a miniature
red-figure representation, from the late 5th c. BC.
Exceptional bronze sculpture are the god Hermes
carrying a ram (*Kriophoros*), 6th c. BC (Case 12), the
nude ephebe (Case 17) and the wonderful roe deer,
5th c. BC (Case 16), as well as the two folding mirrors,
4th c. BC (Cases 24, 25). The renowned sets of jewellery – belts, diadems, necklaces etc. – from Demetrias
(Case 23) and Karpenisi (Cases 26, 27), are superb
examples of the goldsmith's art in Hellenistic times
while the gold *naiskos* with the drunken Dionysos
and the Satyr, in relief, from the 2nd c. BC, is without
parallel (Case 26). The Roman Age is covered by a
series of characteristic pieces of polychrome jewellery

*Attic clay egg model (öon). The game of
Rhabdomancy. By the Washing Painter.
Near Athens. 420-410 BC (no. St. 332).*

*Bronze folding mirror with repre-
sentation of Herakles and Auge.
Peloponnesian workshop. c. 340 BC
(no. St. 312).*

Gold, enamel and pearl earrings with cufic inscription. Crete. 10th-11th c. AD (no. St. 483).

Bronze peacock-shaped lamp. 5th c. AD (no. St. 435).

(Cases 29, 30), the fragments of an excellent bronze relief (Case 32) and the marble female portrait. Especially interesting is the very important collection of Byzantine jewellery (Case 34). Earrings, pectorals, bracelets ets., offer a unique picture of the opulent and extravagant adornment to which Byzantine ladies and imperial dignitaries were accustomed. A selection of bronze and silver Byzantine and Post-byzantine vessels (Cases 35, 36) completes the marvellous spectrum of Greek artist tradition in the Stathatos Collection.

EOS ZERVOUDAKI

Silver bowl with bust of St. Nicholas. 1652 (no. St. 437).

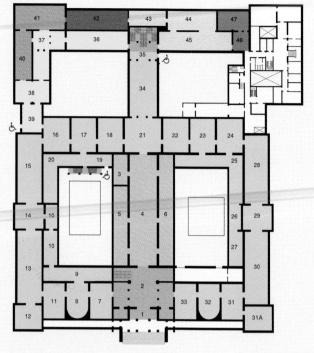

GROUND FLOOR

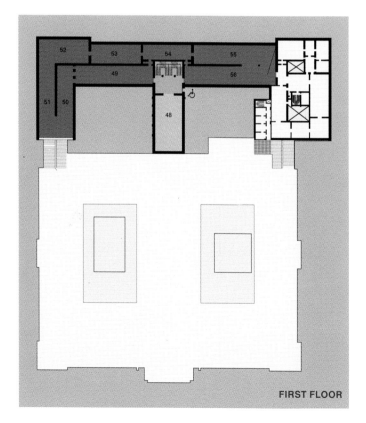

FIRST FLOOR

VESTIBULE

PREHISTORIC COLLECTION

SCULPTURE COLLECTION

BRONZE COLLECTION

EGYPTIAN COLLECTION

VASE AND MINOR OBJECTS
COLLECTION

STATHATOS COLLECTION

TEMPORARY EXHIBITIONS

LECTURE HALL

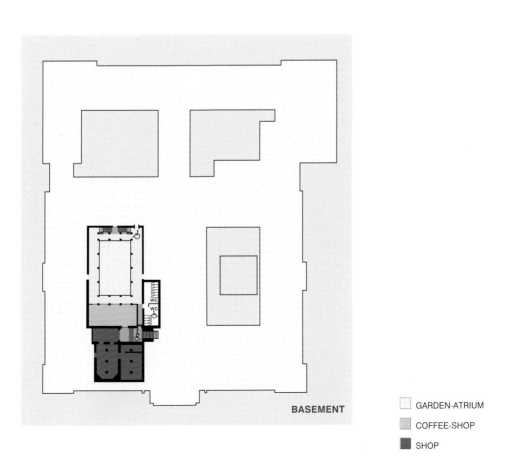

BASEMENT

☐ GARDEN-ATRIUM

■ COFFEE-SHOP

■ SHOP